Focused Moments:
Connecting Through Stories and Mindful Leadership

Danielle Lord, Ph.D.
Anika Klix, M.A. ORGL|HR
2nd Edition

Joy House Publishing, LLC
Federal Way, WA

Copyright © 2025 Danielle Lord, PhD and Anika Klix

All rights reserved. No part of this book may be reproduced, stored in a retrieval system, or transmitted in any form or by any means—electronic, mechanical, photocopying, recording, or otherwise—without the author's or the publisher's prior written permission. Brand and product names are trademarks or registered trademarks of their respective owners.

1st edition Published 2023
Joy House Publishing, LLC
ISBN: 979-8-9907033-2-2

Edited by Anika Klix
Published by Joy House Publishing, LLC
Federal Way, WA

This book is dedicated to people who lead from where they are because everyone is a leader.

Contents

Acknowledgments: Danielle ix

Acknowledgments: Anika x

Foreword xi

Introduction 1

SECTION ONE: INSPIRATIONS 5

   The Power of Imagination 7

   Bridge Builder 9

   The Weather 13

   The Oldest Living Tree 17

   Impossible to Possible 21

   Cologne Cathedral 23

   Far and Wide 27

   Listen 29

   Are You Blessed? 33

   Recognizing the Gift 35

   Who Packs Your Parachute? 37

   The Power of Resilience 39

   What You See Is Not Always What Is 41

   The Blind Men and the Elephant 45

   Stars to Steer By 49

- The One Dollar Miracle 51
- The Tale of Teddy Stoddard 55
- The Window 61
- Spiritual Leader 65

SECTION TWO: LESSONS FROM ANIMALS 69

- In the Pursuit of Excellence 71
- The Power of Team 73
- Stronger Together: The V-Formation 75
- Be the Big Elephant 79
- Trouble on the Ark 83
- Horse & rider | leader & follower 87

SECTION THREE: DEVELOPMENTAL REFLECTIONS 93

- A Winding Path 95
- Mindset Matters 97
- Storytelling 101
- The Power of Perception 103

SECTION FOUR: SCIENCE IN THE REAL WORLD 107

- Pascal's Law and Teams 109
- By Way of the Water 113
- On a mission 117

A Little Stress is Vital for Survival............................ 121
Many Hands Make Light Work 125
SECTION FIVE: MINDFUL LEADERSHIP 129
Definitions 131
Mindful Meetings 133
Cultivating Compassion 145
10 Ways to be More Mindful at Work 149
Mindful Questions for Team Meetings 151
About the Authors 155
DANIELLE 157
ANIKA 159
HOW TO CONTACT US 161
TESTIMONIALS... 162

Acknowledgments: Danielle

Nothing great ever happens alone. It takes a team of people –friends, supporters, loved ones, even those providing constructive feedback—to produce something meaningful. In the second edition of Focused Moments, I am so pleased that my friend Anika Klix joined me to provide more inspiration and reflection through her amazing insights.

I originally wrote Focused Moments to help teams connect or re-connect after months, perhaps even years, of being physically apart during and after the COVID-19 safety measures. I found solace in the quiet days. I learned that chatting with Cat (yes, that's her name), watching the doe sleeping near the camellia and the squirrels chasing each other, and spending time in my yard (even if it was looking out the window) were, in fact, forms of meditation. During this time, I compiled my own list of "reflections" to assemble Focused Moments. Whether it's team connections, meditation, creating new connections, or strengthening relationships, presence is vital and very needed as we collectively move into the future.

To my friends and family who provided support, thank you. Words alone cannot express my gratitude for your ongoing, unwavering support and encouragement.

Acknowledgments: Anika

Had I understood the power of mindfulness when I was younger, I believe I might have avoided much suffering and heartache. But hindsight is 20/20, and I now see that every step of my journey has led me to this moment for a reason. I am deeply grateful for the experiences that have shaped me—the hardships and the blessings.

I owe much to the lessons I've learned in the many roles I've embraced: as a mom, daughter, partner, wife, sister, friend, professional, student, and more. Each role has contributed to my growth and understanding.

To Danielle: Thank you for your unwavering support, friendship, and shared passion for leadership and for championing small businesses and entrepreneurs. Your partnership has been a true gift.

To my friends, family, and chosen family: Thank you for encouraging me to pursue my passions and for being my constant source of strength and inspiration. You know who you are, and I am forever grateful.

Namaste.

Foreword

Awareness, presence, and empowerment inspire mindful and meaningful change. We live in a world bursting with information and know-how. At our fingertips are courses, mentors, websites, and apps to quickly get the information we need. Yet, it is presence and authenticity that propel positive change and powerful living.

For over 25 years, it has been my joy and privilege to support hundreds of aspiring health and wellness coaches to become more self-aware, connect through presence, and fan the flame of their clients' brilliance. Fundamental to mindful coaching is the willingness to step into Not Knowing.

Mindfulness and presence are at the heart of Focused Moments. Through their collaboration, Danielle and Anika demonstrate their dedication to allow inner wisdom to guide their way. They resist the temptation to "tell," and instead use questions, stories, metaphors, and analogies to promote discovery, reflection, and balance.

Thank you, Danielle and Anika, for this thoughtful, heart-inspired book that models and inspires mindfulness and presence.

Billie Frances, M.A., NBC-HWC
Author of Awareness Is Enough: Reflections on Being a Coach

Introduction

The not-so-distant past - December 8, 2015

Our small "formation" cohort arrived at the cemetery at dusk. The December weather, typical of the PNW, was cold, damp, and misty. With Nancy, my friend and colleague, we carried our candles and walked together arm in arm for added warmth. Our heavy wool coats, hats, gloves, and scarves were barely enough to keep out the penetrable damp chill of December.

We approached Mother Joseph's simple headstone, and I gasped at the realization that we were in the cemetery on the 159th Anniversary of their arrival to Fort Vancouver, part of the WA territory. Realizing that these five pioneering women arrived in the same conditions at nearly the same time with little to nothing was an intense moment. Suddenly, the dripped wax on my pants and the pervasive cold no longer seemed to matter.

The distant past - December 8, 1856

Their journey began in late spring. It took the five nuns by coach across Canada from Montreal to New York, where they boarded a ship and sailed around Cape Horn back up through the Pacific Ocean to the Washington Territory. The ship survived an early winter storm in Boiler Bay as they neared their destination. Led by Mother Joseph, the five women were tired, sea-weary, and hungry when they finally arrived near dusk. Having not heard any news of their arrival and fearing they had not survived the recent storm, the bishop was not at the port to greet them. Through the dark, damp, drizzle, cold, and mud, they found their way to Fort Vancouver; even the attic that would be their temporary dwelling had not been cleaned out.

Over several years, these same five women would embark on a journey that would take them across the Pacific Northwest territories, building many hospitals that served the area's pioneers to form the first Corporation of the Washington territory, even pre-dating statehood. The Sisters of Providence would leave a legacy of healthcare spread across five states and over 65,000 employees in that 159-year span, which continues today.

The present – December 2024

I began my 13-year tenure with Providence in 2004. At that time, the few remaining Sisters of Providence sought ways to ensure their legacy would survive them. They had recently implemented "reflections," short stories, quotes, and quips shared at the beginning of every meeting. The idea was that physical presence was not enough. Doing the work of Providence required mental and emotional presence as well.

I recall the first non-Providence meeting I attended. I couldn't figure out why I felt so disjointed, disconnected, and discombobulated...only to realize that the meeting did not include a reflection. It was at that point, realizing the power of presence, that I took reflections much more seriously.

Presence is powerful—not just physically but mentally and emotionally, something I still strive to perfect. Presence allows us to take in and read the emotions of the room, listen to respond, not react, and allow others to express themselves fully and freely. I am so excited to partner with my friend Anika, who added a section on mindfulness and team connections to this second edition of Focused Moments.

Over my remaining years and roles at Providence, I got to know those five pioneering women quite well. Though they had long passed, their lives and experiences shared through stories and their resilience through struggles and challenges were the material for many of my reflections. As such, I amassed quite a collection of stories over the years while participating in the maturation of the reflections within Providence, many of them shared with you in Focused Moments. I hope you enjoy this collection of old and new stories as you develop your sense of presence with yourself, create community through stories, and deepen connections with others. In the words of one of the last remaining Sisters of Providence, Sister Suzanne, "You're exactly where you're supposed to be at this moment in time."

Danielle

Danielle Lord, PhD
Archetype Learning Solutions

Focused Moments

SECTION ONE: INSPIRATIONS

Lessons are all around us. From the simple to the complex, events shape and reshape our perspectives. The following pages include various stories, from the silly and funny to the more severe and dramatic. Take time to reflect and to discuss.

Focused Moments

The Power of Imagination

Focused moments can inspire creativity, open up dialogue, allow one to focus or meditate, and more.

What comes to mind as you spend time with this photo?

_____
_____

What did you see first? Was it one thing or the whole picture?

_____
_____

How does the picture make you feel?

_____
_____

Focused Moments

JOURNAL SPACE

How have you used inspiration, creativity, mediation, and conversation to enhance your relationships or collaboration?

Bridge Builder

Without bridges, the best-built roads lead nowhere. The most impressive visions remain invisible, and the best-laid plans fail. In life and work, a connection is everything. You build bridges; you make connections.

Discussion questions:

1. How do you build bridges in your work, home, or within the larger community you call home?
2. How do you mend bridges when they fall into disrepair?
3. What is the best bridge-building strategy that you have used?

JOURNAL SPACE

A wintery scene of fog and frosty trees

What comes to mind for you when you see this scene?

"The world of reality has its limits; the world of imagination is boundless."

– Jean-Jacques Rousseau

The Weather

I've come to the frightening conclusion that I am the decisive element in the workplace. It is my daily mood that makes the weather. As a leader, I possess a tremendous power to make an employee's life miserable or joyous. I can be a tool of torture or a spark of inspiration. I can humiliate or humor, hurt or heal. In all situations, my response influences whether a crisis will be escalated or de-escalated, and some will be humanized or dehumanized.

---

[1] Source: Dr. Haim Ginott, N.d.

Discussion questions:

1. When have you influenced someone's behavior or someone's day?
2. Was it negative or positive?
3. Do leaders have an ethical imperative to create inspiration and safety? Why or why not?

Connecting through stories and mindful leadership

JOURNAL SPACE

The sun rising in Tianjin city

How many sunrises have you experienced?

Do you prefer sunrise or sunset? Why?

"Stories of imagination tend to upset those without one."

– Terry Pratchett

The Oldest Living Tree

This not-very-tall spruce tree (only five meters in height) has been standing on a ridge of the Fulufjället Mountain in Sweden for over nine thousand years. It was already ancient when the Egyptians started building the great Pyramids far away in the warm south.

The Roman Empire grew and fell to nothing while the tree slowly matured. It has kept going in the face of appalling weather in quiet obedience to the same basic forces that have always governed its existence: rain, sunlight, wind, and the nutrients it imperceptibly draws from the forbidding rocky soil beneath it.

---

[2] Source: The School of Life, 2018

Discussion questions:

1. When did you have to bloom where you were planted?
2. How do you withstand appalling weather?
3. What would you share with others who face adversity?

Connecting through stories and mindful leadership

JOURNAL SPACE

**Mac and cheese: everyone's favorite food, or is it?
Is that bacon?**

What is your comfort food?

What memories does it bring up?

"Logic will get you from A to B. Imagination will take you everywhere."

– Albert Einstein

Impossible to Possible

In Germany, experts provide that if trains went as fast as 15 miles per hour – considered a frightful speed – blood would spurt from the noses of travelers, and passengers would suffocate when going through tunnels. In the United States, experts said the introduction of the railroad would require the building of many insane asylums since people would be terrified at the sight of the locomotives.

The New York YMCA announced typing lessons for women in 1881, and vigorous protests erupted because the female constitution would break from the strain.

When the idea of iron ships was proposed, experts insisted that they would not float, that they would damage more quickly than wooden ships when grounding, that it would be challenging to preserve the bottom from rust, and that the iron would wreak havoc with the compass readings.

New Jersey farmers resisted the first successful cast-iron plow invented in 1797, claiming cast iron would poison the land and stimulate the growth of weeds.

Don't let the word impossible stop you. If inventors and visionaries undone every impossible task, our lives would be considerably more difficult. Nothing worth doing is impossible!

---

[3] Source: God's Little Devotional Book, 2001.

Focused Moments

Discussion questions:

1. Sometimes, we are our own worst critics. How do you quiet the voice in your head and move forward?
2. What about the voices of so-called "experts"?
3. How do you create the possible?

Cologne Cathedral

When our work feels interminable, we should turn our thoughts to the Cologne Cathedral for strength and patience. Construction began in 1248 but paused in 1473 when funds ran out. It started in 1842 and finished in 1880, 632 years after things started (the event marked by a nationwide celebration headed up by Emperor Wilhelm I). However, it wasn't the end because WWII created a whole new round of damage, so much of it that construction continues today. Only in 2007 did the Cathedral acquire a new stained-glass window by Gerhard Richter. What is incredible is that the Cathedral is magnificent and will be sublime when finished. The best things tend to take a lot of time.

---

[4] Source: The School of Life, 2018.

Discussion questions:

1. What has been your Cologne Cathedral?
2. How do you demonstrate patience during events that are longer or more difficult than expected?
3. How do you treasure things and people that have stood the test of time?

Connecting through stories and mindful leadership

JOURNAL SPACE

An Autumnal Walk in the Woods

Where is your favorite place to take a walk?

Do you have a seasonal preference?

"You can't use up creativity. The more you use, the more you have."

– Maya Angelou

Far and Wide

The positive actions you take do not stop with you. Many of them go on and on, far beyond you, to people and places you will never know about.

The value you create does not end with you. It sets the stage for more positive value and then for even more value.

Somewhere today, someone's life has been made better because of a positive action you have taken in the past. In some way, the world is becoming a better place because of something you did weeks, months, or even years ago.

You can never know or control how far and wide your actions will extend. You can, however, control the nature of those actions.

The more love, kindness, and thoughtfulness you put into your actions, the more positively those actions will multiply and radiate out into the world. Put the best of yourself into all you do and your unique value will be spread far and wide.

Your influence on life is immensely greater than it may appear on the surface. Live each moment with goodness, truth, and integrity; in more ways than you can realize, you'll be making the world a better place.

Discussion questions:

---

[5] Source: Ralph Marston, N.d.

Focused Moments

1. How do you use positive actions to help influence?
2. What specific behaviors or actions do you take for positive influence?
3. How do you recognize what you can and cannot control?
4. How do you let go of the things you cannot control?

Listen

Listening is very hard because it requires so much interior stability that we no longer need to prove ourselves through speeches, arguments, statements, or declarations. True listeners no longer have an inner need to make their presence known. They are free to receive, welcome, and accept.

Listening is much more than allowing another to talk while waiting for a chance to respond. Listening is paying full attention to others and welcoming them into our very beings. The beauty of listening is that those who are listened to start feeling accepted, start taking their words more seriously and discover their true selves. Listening is a form of spiritual hospitality that invites strangers to become friends, get to know their inner selves more fully, and even dare to be silent with you.

---

[6] Source: Henri Y. A. Nouwin, N.d.

Discussion questions:

1. How do you demonstrate active listening?
2. Have you ever felt fully heard?
3. What was that experience like, and how can you provide that for others?

JOURNAL SPACE

Mossy rocks and cascade mountain streams

What is the first thing you notice about this photo?

_____
_____
_____
_____
_____
_____
_____
_____
_____
_____
_____
_____

"Kindness is the language which the deaf can hear, and the blind can see."

– Mark Twain

Are You Blessed?

If you woke up with more health than illness this morning, you are more blessed than the million who will not survive this week.

Suppose you have never experienced the danger of battle, the loneliness of imprisonment, the agony of torture, or the pangs of starvation. In that case, you are ahead of 500 million people worldwide.

If you have food in the refrigerator, clothes on your back, a roof overhead, and a place to sleep, you are richer than 75% of the world's population.

If you have money in the bank, in your wallet, and spare change in a dish somewhere…you are among the top 8% of the world's wealth.

You are rare if your parents are still alive and married, especially in the United States.

If you hold up your head with a smile and are truly thankful, you are blessed because the majority can, but most do not.

If you can read, you are more blessed than over two billion people worldwide who cannot read at all.

---

[7] Source: Bill Greer, Chicken Soup for the Veteran's Soul, 2007

Discussion questions:

1. How are you blessed?
2. What two things about this message were most compelling?
3. How can you use this to inspire others?

Recognizing the Gift

According to legend, a young man roaming the desert came across a spring of delicious, crystal-clear water. The water was very sweet, so he filled his canteen to take some back to a tribal elder who had been his teacher. After a four-day journey, he presented the water to the old man, who took a deep drink, smiled warmly, and thanked the student lavishly for the water.

Later, the teacher presented the water to another student. The young student spat out the water, saying it was awful. It had become stale during the journey in the old leather container.

The student challenged the teacher, "Master, the water was foul. Why did you pretend to like it?"

The teacher replied, "You only tasted the water, I tasted the gift. The water was simply the container for an act of loving-kindness, and nothing could be sweeter."

Discussion questions:

1. When did you realize that something, a bad experience or a disappointment, was actually a gift?
2. What "gifts" do you bring?
3. How do you honor the uniqueness of the gifts of others?

Who Packs Your Parachute?

Charles Plumb was a Navy jet pilot. On his seventy-sixth combat mission, his plane was shot down, and he parachuted into enemy territory, where he was captured and spent six years as a prisoner of war. He survived and now lectures on the lessons he learned from his experiences.

One day, a man approached Plumb and his wife in a restaurant and asked, "Are you the Navy pilot, Plumb"?

"Yes, how did you know?" Plumb responded.

"I packed your parachute," the man replied.

Plumb was amazed and grateful, telling him, "If the chute you packed hadn't worked, I wouldn't be here today!"

Plumb refers to this in his lectures, his realization that the anonymous sailors who packed the parachutes held the pilots' lives in their hands. Yet, the pilots never gave these sailors a second thought, not even a hello, let alone express gratitude.

---

[8] Source: Industrial Resources News; Who Packs Your Parachute: A True Story About Charles Plumb, 2016

Discussion questions:

1. Who packs your parachute?
2. Who helps you through life, perhaps even silently, without acknowledgment or expressing gratitude?
3. When was the last time you expressed gratitude?

The Power of Resilience

One day, a farmer's donkey fell into a well. The animal cried and brayed piteously for hours as the farmer tried to figure out what to do. Finally, he decided the animal was old and the well needed to be covered up anyway. It just wasn't worth it to retrieve the donkey.

He invited all his neighbors to come over and help him. They all grabbed shovels and began shoveling dirt into the well. At first, the donkey, realizing what was happening, cried horribly. Then, to everyone's amazement, he quieted.

A few shovel-loads later, the farmer finally looked down into the well. He was astonished at what he saw. The donkey was doing something amazing with each shovel of dirt that hit his back. He would shake off each shovel of dirt and take a step up! Everyone was amazed when, eventually, the donkey stepped over the edge and happily trotted off!

Life is going to shovel dirt on you—lots of dirt! The trick to getting out of the well is shaking it off and stepping up. Each of our troubles is a steppingstone. We can get out of the deepest of wells through resilience, experience, and not giving in. Shake it off and take a step up.

Discussion questions:

1. When has life shoveled dirt on you? How did you demonstrate resilience?
2. Have you ever been in a tricky situation and taken time to assess the situation to see if there was a better way out? How did that help your situation?
3. Is there a situation that felt disparaging, but you could happily trot off in the end?

What You See Is Not Always What Is

Two battleships assigned to a training squadron sat off the coast of California for several days. The weather was heavy and challenging during that time. The captain noticed the patchy fog as night fell and remained on the bridge.

Shortly after dark, the lookout on the wing of the bridge reported, "Flashing light. Bearing on the starboard bow."

"Is it steady or moving astern?" asked the captain.

The lookout replied, "Steady, Captain," which meant

---

[9] Source: Lighthouse and naval vessel urban legend. (2022, December 5). Wikipedia.
https://en.wikipedia.org/wiki/Lighthouse_and_naval_vessel_urban_legend

that the ship was on a collision course with another ship.

The captain called to the signalman, "Signal that ship. Advise that you alter course 20 degrees."

The answering signal replied, "Advisable that you change course 20 degrees."

The captain said, "Send another message. I am a Senior Captain. Change course 20 degrees."

"I am a Seaman Second Class sir," came the reply. "Change your course at once!"

The captain, now furious, spat out, "We are a battleship squadron. Change your course 20 degrees!"

The flashing light replied, "I am a lighthouse."

Discussion questions:

1. When were you faced with a lighthouse moment?
2. Has there been a time when you had an expectation or an assumption only to find that you were incorrect?
3. If so, how did you make amends?

Focused Moments

"We are like islands in the sea, separate on the surface but connected in the deep."

– William James

The Blind Men and the Elephant

A story of perception, truth, perspective, empathy, communication, and understanding

Six blind men were discussing exactly what they believed an elephant to be. Although each had heard how strange the creature was, none had ever seen one before. So, the blind men agreed to find an elephant and discover what the animal was like. It did not take the men long to find an elephant at a nearby market.

The first blind man approached the beast and patted the animal's firm flat side. "It seems to me," he said, "that the elephant is just like a wall."

The second blind man reached out and touched the tusks of the elephant. "No, this is round, smooth, and sharp – the elephant is a spear," he stated.

The third blind man stepped forward, touching the elephant's trunk. "Well, I can't agree with either of you.

I feel something squirming so surely the elephant is like a snake," he stated.

The fourth blind man, now very puzzled, reached out to feel the elephant's leg. "You're all talking complete nonsense," he said. "The elephant is just like a tree!"

Touching the elephant's large ears, the fifth blind man exclaimed, "This is clearly a fan!"

The sixth blind man approached and touched the tail of the great elephant. He stated that the rest were mad and stated, "It is clearly a rope."

All six men continued arguing, basing their reality on their experiences. It was an argument they would never win or resolve as each was concerned only with their perspective. None of them could step back to fully see the point of view of the others or the whole picture. Each man felt something quite different and formulated an image in their mind's eye, and while, in part, each man was correct, none was wholly correct.

There is never just one way to look at something. Perceptions differ depending on who is seeing.

*Note: This story has various versions, most based on legends from multiple Southeast Asian and Indian cultures. Some claim it is thousands of years old.

Discussion questions:

1. Has there been a time when you were at odds with another person only to realize that there was a different perspective? How did you handle it?

2. Did it cloud your judgment about the person, or did a previous judgment about that person influence your perspective?

3. When others have not been able to see something visible to you, what methods of communication have you used to help others see a different or whole part of something?

JOURNAL SPACE

There is no better sound than the belly laughs of an infant

What do you think of when you see this picture or think about a laughing baby?

Stars to Steer By

May we break down boundaries, tear down walls, and build on the foundation of goodness.

May we look past differences, gain understanding, and embrace acceptance.

May we reach out to each other rather than resist.

May we be better stewards of the Earth, protecting, nurturing, and replenishing the beauty of nature.

May we practice gratitude for all we have rather than complain about our needs.

May we seek cures for the sick, help for the hungry, and love for the lonely.

May we share our talents, give our time, and teach our children.

May we tenderly hold hope for the future in our hearts and do all we can to build a bright tomorrow.

May we LOVE with our whole hearts, for that's the only way to love.

Discussion questions:

1. Which of the nine sentiments listed appeals to you most and why?
2. Which do you find most challenging?
3. Which would you be most grateful for?

The One Dollar Miracle

A little girl went to her bedroom and pulled a jelly jar from its hiding place in the closet. She poured the change onto the floor and counted it carefully... thrice. The total had to be exactly perfect, with no chance for mistakes. Carefully placing the coins back in the jar and twisting on the cap, she slipped out the back door, making her way to the Rexall Drugstore with the big, red Indian Chief above the door.

She waited patiently for the pharmacist to give her some attention, but he was too busy then. She twisted her feet to make some scuffling noises and cleared her throat with the most disgusting sound she could. Finally, she took a quarter from the jar and placed it firmly on the counter.

"And what do you want?" the seemingly annoyed pharmacist asked. "I'm talking to my brother from Chicago, whom I haven't seen in ages," he said without waiting for a reply.

"Well, I want to talk to you about my brother," the girl replied. He's really, really sick, and I want to buy a miracle."

"I beg your pardon?" replied the pharmacist.

"His name is Andrew, and he has something bad

---

[10] Source: The Price of a Miracle. (2022, December 5). Lamplighter. https://lamplighter.net/c/moments/thie-price-of-a-mirace/

growing inside his head. My daddy says only a miracle can save him now. So, how much does a miracle cost?"

Softening his tone, the pharmacist replied, "I'm sorry I can't help you. We don't sell miracles here."

"But I have money to pay for it. If it's not enough, I can work for more. Just please tell me how much it will cost," the girl pleaded.

The pharmacist's brother, a well-dressed man, stooped down to ask the girl, "What type of miracle does your brother need?"

"I don't know," replied the girl as tears welled up in her eyes. "I just know he's sick and mommy says he needs an operation, and daddy says we can't pay for it. I want to use my money to help."

"How much do you have?" inquired the man from Chicago.

The barely audible girl answered, "One dollar and eleven cents. It's all the money I have."

"Well, that's a coincidence," said the man from Chicago. "One dollar and eleven cents is exactly the price of a miracle for brothers."

The well-dressed man from Chicago was Dr. Carlton Armstrong, a neurosurgeon who completed the operation free of charge. While Andrew was recovering, their parents discussed the chain of events and wondered what such a miracle cost.

The girl smiled because she knew one dollar and eleven cents!

Discussion questions:

1. The little girl in the story had little to give, yet the illustrious surgeon took what little money she did have. Why?
2. When have you been able to provide a clandestine miracle for someone in need?
3. Do miracles need to cost money?

Focused Moments

JOURNAL SPACE

What fun little wooden pigs!

What quirky things do you like and make you smile?

_____
_____
_____
_____
_____
_____
_____
_____
_____
_____
_____
_____

The Tale of Teddy Stoddard

On the very first day of school that fall, Mrs. Thompson stood in front of her fifth-grade class and told a lie. Like most teachers, she looked at her pupils and said that she loved them all and would treat them alike. However, it was impossible because there in front of her, slumped in his seat in the third row, was a little boy named Teddy Stoddard.

Mrs. Thompson had watched Teddy the year before and noticed he didn't play well with the other children. His clothes were unkempt, and he constantly needed a bath; he was unpleasant. It got to the point during the first few months that she would take delight in marking his papers with a broad red pen, making bold Xs and then a big F at the top of the paper.

Because Teddy was a sullen boy, no one else seemed to enjoy him either. At the school where Mrs. Thompson taught, she was required to review each child's school records and put off Teddy's for last. When she opened his file, she was quite surprised.

His first-grade teacher wrote, "Teddy is a bright, inquisitive child with a ready laugh. He does his work neatly and has good manners. He is a joy to be around."

His second-grade teacher wrote, "Teddy is an excellent student and well-liked by his classmates. He

---

[11] Source: Ripple Kindness Project. (n.d.), The Teddy Stoddard Story – Read by Dr. Wayne Dyer. https://ripplekindness.org/the-teddy-stoddard-story/

is troubled, however, because his mother has a terminal illness, and life at home must be a struggle."

His third-grade teacher wrote, "Teddy continues to work hard, but his mother's death has been hard on him. He tries to do his best, but his father doesn't show much interest, and his home life will soon affect him if some steps aren't taken."

His fourth-grade teacher wrote, "Teddy is withdrawn and doesn't show much interest in school. He doesn't have many friends and sometimes falls asleep in class. He is frequently tardy and could become a problem."

By then, Mrs. Thompson realized the issue, but Christmas was coming fast. With the school play and all, it wasn't until the day before the holidays began that she was suddenly forced to focus on Teddy Stoddard.

Her students brought her presents, all in beautiful ribbon and bright paper, except for Teddy's, which was clumsily wrapped in the heavy, brown paper grocery bag. Mrs. Thompson took pains to open it in the middle of the other gifts. Some of the children started to laugh when they saw a rhinestone bracelet with some of the stones missing, and a bottle that was one-quarter full of perfume. She stifled the children's laughter by proclaiming how pretty the bracelet was, putting it on, and dabbing some of the perfume on her wrist.

Teddy stayed behind long enough to say, "Mrs. Thompson, today you smelled just like my mom used to." After the children left, she cried for at least an hour. On that very day, she quit teaching reading, writing, and math and began teaching children.

Mrs. Thompson paid particular attention to the kid they called "Teddy." As she worked with him, his mind seemed to come alive. The more she encouraged him, the faster he responded. On the days before an important test, Mrs. Thompson would remember the perfume. By the end of the year, he had become one of the smartest children in the class and had also become the pet of the teacher who had once vowed to love all children the same.

A year later, she found a note under her door from Teddy, telling her that she was his favorite out of all the elementary school teachers he'd had.

Six years passed before she received another note from Teddy. He wrote that he had finished high school, was third in his class, and that she was still his favorite teacher.

Four years later, another letter said that while things had been tough at times, he'd stayed in school and would graduate from college with the highest of honors. He assured Mrs. Thompson that she was still his favorite teacher.

Then, four more years passed, and yet another letter came. This time, he explained that he had decided to go further after getting his bachelor's degree. The letter explained that she was still his favorite teacher; this time, it was a little longer; it was signed, -**Theodore F. Stoddard, MD.**

Discussion questions:

1. We never really know the impact we'll have on the life of another. What impact has someone had on you?
2. How did that impact change your life timeline?
3. Like Mrs. Thompson, what steps can you take to ensure you positively affect someone else's life?

Connecting through stories and mindful leadership

JOURNAL SPACE

A simple mud puddle

What would you do if you came across a puddle covering your path?

_____
_____
_____
_____
_____
_____
_____
_____
_____
_____

Focused Moments

"The wound is the place where the Light enters you."

– Rumi

The Window

Two men, both seriously ill, occupied the same hospital room. One man was allowed to sit in his bed for an hour daily to drain the fluids from his lungs. His bed was next to the only window. The other man had to spend all of his time on his back.

The men talked for hours on end. They spoke of their wives and families, their homes, jobs, military service, and where they had vacationed. Every afternoon, when the man by the window could sit up, he'd describe to his roommate all he could see through the window.

The man in the other bed lived for those one-hour periods when the world would be broadened and enlivened by all the activity and color of the outside world. The man had said the window overlooked a park with a lovely lake. Ducks and swans played on the water while children sailed their model boats. Lovers walked arm-in-arm amid flowers of every color. Grand old trees graced the landscape, and a fine view of the city skyline could be seen in the distance. As the man by the window described all of this in exquisite detail, the man on the other side of the room would close his eyes and imagine the picturesque scene.

One warm afternoon, the man by the window described a parade passing by. Although the other man

---

[12] Source: Moral Stories 26. (2022, December 5). The Window Story for Inspiration. https://moralstories26.com/the-window-story-for-inspiration/

could not hear the band, he could see it in his mind's eye as the gentleman by the window portrayed it with descriptive words.

Unexpectedly, a strange thought entered his head: "Why should he have the pleasure of seeing everything while I get to see nothing"? It didn't seem fair.

As the thought fermented, the man felt ashamed. As the days passed and he missed even more sights, his envy eroded into resentment and soon turned sour. He began to brood and found himself unable to sleep. He should be near that window – and that thought began to control his life.

Late one night, as he lay awake staring at the ceiling, the man by the window began to cough. He was choking on the fluids in his lungs. The other man watched in the dimly lit room as the struggling man by the window groped for the call button. Listening from across the room, he never moved or pushed his call button, which would have brought the nurse running. In less than five minutes, the coughing and the choking stopped, along with the sound of breathing. Now, there was only silence.

The following morning, the day nurse arrived to bring water for their baths. When she found the lifeless body of the man by the window, she was saddened and called for the attendant to take him away – no words, no fuss. As soon as it seemed appropriate, the man asked if he could be moved next to the window. The nurse was happy to make the switch, and after making sure he was comfortable, she left him alone.

He slowly, painfully propped himself up on one elbow to take his first look. Finally, he would have the joy of seeing it all himself. He strained to turn to look out of the window slowly.

It faced a blank wall.

Discussion questions:

1. Keeping a positive attitude is sometimes the most challenging part of life, especially during difficult situations. How do you maintain a positive attitude when all else feels bleak?

2. How do you see resiliency and/or mindfulness playing a role in patient #1?

3. It's often said that "ignorance is bliss." Has there been a time when you were disappointed by reality? If so, what did you do to re-frame the situation?

Spiritual Leader

Spiritual leaders can help shape an achievable, clear, and compelling vision that conveys where an organization is going, where employees are heading, and why they should be proud of its direction. At its core is the organization's mission.

Vision, values, and determination add soul to the organization. Without them, organizations react but do not create. They forecast but do not imagine. They analyze but do not question. They act but do not strive.

Leaders with vision love what they do and care passionately about sharing a vision. Their soaring ideals and values are gifts that, in spirit, set fire to the hearts of others as they shape and live the realities of a vision.

---

[13] Source: Timothy Brown and Patricia Sullivan, N.d.

Discussion questions:

1. Is there a place for spirituality in leadership?
2. Why or why not?
3. How does spirituality connect to a compelling vision?

JOURNAL SPACE

The sounds of the beach

What is the first sound you remember when you think of the beach?

Focused Moments

SECTION TWO:
LESSONS FROM ANIMALS

Animals can teach us a lot about teamwork and leadership. The beautiful thing about animals is their absence of ego; they care only about the ecosystem and the survival of the whole. As humans in organizations, the survival of the whole is the survival of our organizations as leaders or individual contributors. The following pages are just a few examples.

Focused Moments

In the Pursuit of Excellence

Known for their strength in flight, bald eagles are among the most majestic creatures in the sky. With power and balance, they fly miles above the Earth, catching warm air currents to lift them thousands of feet into the air. Their keen vision allows them to see far-off challenges, and they soar through each pursuit with great success.

JOURNAL SPACE

There is something very majestic about a deer stag

What is your first thought when you look at this photo?

The Power of Team

The flightless fairy penguin of Australia stands less than a foot tall and is clumsy on land where the fox is its natural enemy. Alone, one penguin won't survive long. So, at the end of each day in the water, they gather where the surf meets the shore, waiting until the last penguin joins them. Then, shoulder to shoulder, they march up the beach to their burrows. They support one another and rely on each other. Everyone except the fox wins.

JOURNAL SPACE

Ah, the cunning red fox!

When you see a fox, where does your mind take you?

Stronger Together: The V-Formation

The V-formation utilized by geese improves efficiency over long migratory routes and conserves their energy. Each bird flies slightly higher than the bird in front of it, reducing wind resistance. Each bird flies in the upwash of wind from the bird in front, reducing their drag and increasing their range by 71%. The birds flying at the tips and front of the V-shape are rotated in a timely cycleway.

The V-formation conserves the energy and efficiency of the group's energy consumption. As the bird flaps their wings, the air rolls off the wing tip and creates a downwash as the air behind it pushes upward. If you observe the flight pattern, one side of the V is almost always longer than the V-formation. The lead bird tires more quickly, rotating to the back of the formation. If a goose falls out of formation, it suddenly feels drag and resistance, and the goose will quickly return to the proper formation.

Through teamwork, geese can fly a great distance. They stay together to protect and support each other. When they tire, their unity and honking further support them.

Most birds fly quietly, but geese honk loudly to encourage each other to keep up their speed and altitude. Geese are helpful to each other, and their honking sounds encourage the gaggle. The honking also helps to provide a sense of direction and coordinate position changes.

In the summer or early autumn heat, they often make their flights at night. The night air is cooler, which helps to ensure that they do not overheat. Geese do not soar, so they are constantly flapping.

Two additional geese will descend if a goose needs to take a break or is wounded. The loyal goose partners will stay with the other goose until it's better and can fly again.

Connecting through stories and mindful leadership

Discussion questions:

1. Why do animals seem to work together better than people?

2. What inspiration can you draw from animals' intuitive support for one another?

3. How can you be more supportive of your team members?

"In the presence of animals, we learn the value of silent connection and unspoken trust."

– Unknown

Be the Big Elephant

The Pilanesberg Wildlife Reserve adopted several baby elephants orphaned in South Africa. The baby elephants were orphaned because poachers killed their mothers. Shortly after their arrival, they began to exhibit very uncharacteristic elephant behavior; they appeared to be throwing temper tantrums. They acted very aggressively towards the reserve team members, running into the brush, sulking, screaming, and refusing to eat. They refused to leave the brush until hunger eventually brought them out. The baby elephants eventually surrounded and killed several young, endangered white rhinoceros.

The close-knit family unit is fundamental in elephant culture. Adult elephants model the way and demonstrate acceptable herd behavior. To curb the out-

---

[14] Source: Lauren Jackson, Senior HS ASB project, 2013.

of-control elephant babies, six adult males were introduced to re-socialize them. The adult males could intercede several times and re-direct the baby elephant's behavior.

Without role models, there is no example of compassion and empathy, setting acceptable limits, and re-direction, which is one reason things can go wrong. Be the big elephant and model the way.

Discussion questions:

1. When did you have to be the big elephant?
2. What life lessons do we learn as we mature?
3. Can we have a close-knit organizational family?

Focused Moments

"Walk as if you are kissing the Earth with your feet."

— Thích Nhất Hạnh

Trouble on the Ark

Life on the Ark was getting a bit boring. Noah and his animals had spent so many days secluded that they began organizing games and activities to amuse themselves. But with all that pent-up energy, the games got rather rowdy. The woodpecker ended up drilling a hole in the bottom of the Ark. As the water began flooding the boat, the hole got bigger, more water came in, and things got a bit worrisome.

One by one, different animals tried to fix the hole. They eventually got competitive because everyone wanted to be the animal that saved the Ark. The beaver built a dam over the hole, but not even that worked. Everyone was scared and worried that the boat would sink. That was until a bee started talking. The bee explained to everyone how bees always worked together as a team, each doing their best job.

The animals worked together on hearing this, each playing their part by contributing their unique talent. The birds grabbed onto parts of the ark with their beaks and flapped their wings furiously, lifting the boat a little. The elephants sucked up the water with their trunks and shot it back into the sea. The fastest animals ran here and there, collecting materials. Those who made nests took the materials and stuffed them quickly into the hole.

Working together, the animals reduced the amount

---

[15] Source: Pedro Pablo Sacristan, N.d.

of water entering the Ark, but they still hadn't stopped it completely. Desperate, they kept asking each other if any other animals could help. They searched, but no other animals were left in the Ark.

Suddenly, a little fish swam through the hole. The animals realized they still had not asked for help from the sea creatures. They asked the little fish to go and summon help to save their boat. He swam off, and soon, fish after fish, arrived at the Ark. Even a big whale came, and it pressed its great belly against the hole in the ship. This stopped more water from entering, giving the animals on the Ark time to close the hole!

Discussion questions:

1. When did some fun antics develop into a more serious situation? What did you do to get things back on track?
2. How does the power of many minds help develop a more holistic solution?
3. "The one to save the _____!" Have you experienced this, and how did it impact the ability to move forward?

"Leadership is not about being in charge. It is about taking care of those in your charge."

– Simon Sinek

Horse & rider | leader & follower

In the wild, horses are prey. Over millions of years, they have developed keen instincts to keep them safe. Even horses as pets remain hyper-vigilant in their human-designed habitat, which can greatly benefit their humans and others.

Perched atop my pretty Welsh Arab mare in my prized English saddle, I set out on the old logging road that cut through my parents' acreage. It ran alongside the pasture and creek, a remnant of logging, the once economic backbone of WA State. The road ended in a now pasteurized cul-de-sac with three familiar choices. Strait ahead, a road so over-grown navigating it was a curious impossibility. To the right, just beyond the huge oak tree, a shorter road, suitable for cantering with two downed trees – perfect for jumping. This was about a 30-minute ride connected to the dead-end on the only side road of our long dirt road. To the left, a longer trail wide open for several feet, descending into a thick canopy of woods that abutted the very end of the 154th Court in rural Gig Harbor, about an hour's ride overall.

Choosing to go to the left, my horse, familiar with the trail, calmly walked on as indicated by her ears. The snap of a twig, however, changed all of that as she stopped, ears perked forward, followed by a slight nicker that made me take notice. There is an old saying in riding: always let the horse know you're in charge, and plenty of horses have tested this theory with a new rider. At 11 years old and alone in the woods, I had two choices: fight it out or listen to what she could only tell me through her language.

How is riding like leading? Sometimes, we need to listen to the horse −or employee—those closest to the work, knowledgeable of the situation, or with a general awareness not necessarily known to the leader. What is not being said out loud? Do you listen? Do you encourage dialogue? Do you step back, follow, and allow them to lead?

We tend to think about followership as a weakness in leadership. But what if it was actually a position of strength? What if knowing when to step aside and let another lead was the opportunity for a better outcome or safety? What if being a follower provided a team member with a development opportunity rather than simply doing more of the same? What if being a follower meant learning something new that could benefit the team or the organization? Sometimes, we need to be comfortable with knowing when to lead and when to follow.

Focused Moments

Questions to reflect on:

If you're quiet, the unspoken is all around. What is it telling you? When have you been quiet as a leader, and what have you experienced?

Have you experienced when the formal leader should have stepped into a follower role? What was the situation and final results?

How can being a follower enhance projects and outcomes?

Connecting through stories and mindful leadership

JOURNAL SPACE

Silly dog!

What is your immediate reaction?

Focused Moments

SECTION THREE: DEVELOPMENTAL REFLECTIONS

Taking a step back and reflecting is one of the most powerful learning and development tools in our learning journey. The following are a few focused moments from the "Begin from Within" series modules, available on the Archetype Learning Solutions website.

Focused Moments

A Winding Path

It is often said that the path to personal leadership development is winding. Why not a nice, straight line without any obstacles? Why take time to reflect?

How can dedicated, focused time help our personal or leadership development?

_____
_____
_____
_____
_____
_____
_____

Focused Moments

JOURNAL SPACE

A day at the beach, lake, or river

What is your favorite body of water?

Where would you spend your day, and what would you be doing?

Mindset Matters

Consider a time when you had a great idea, something exciting to share, or a new and unique approach to an existing problem. How did others respond?

Questions to reflect on:

Consider a negative response:

What did the receiver do that made it negative?

_____
_____

How did you feel?

_____

What transpired as a result?

_____
_____

Consider a positive response:

What did the receiver do that made it positive?

_____
_____

Focused Moments

How did you feel?

_____

_____

What transpired as a result?

_____

_____

Connecting through stories and mindful leadership

JOURNAL SPACE

Behold the cupcake!

What is being celebrated?

"A leader's ability to imagine the future inspires others to help create it."

– John C. Maxwell

Storytelling

As leaders, why is understanding our learning needs and those of our team members important? How does it serve the team or the organization? How does it relate to a growth or fixed mindset?

Questions to reflect on:

What was the last powerful story that you heard?

What was the impact, and what did you learn?

How were you influenced?

Did it provide you with a new perspective?

Focused Moments

JOURNAL SPACE

Classic vinyl

What would be the next record on your turntable?

_____
_____
_____
_____
_____
_____
_____
_____
_____
_____
_____

Connecting through stories and mindful leadership

The Power of Perception

We tend to use our perception as a bias to support our truth. We work hard to believe our own stories; perception is no different. We naturally believe that how we see the world is closer to the truth than how others see it. In other words, we all have a slightly different reality.

Perception is "attaching meaning to the information we take in through our senses."

When you look at the two images above, what comes to mind?

Our brain works very quickly. It generates automatic thoughts based on things we see or our perceptions. These thoughts pop in based on our observations and can expand or limit our ability to interact effectively with others. As leaders, this can damage self, team members, teams, and organizational goals. We can also use different perceptions to be curious, enhance discussion, and alter outcomes.

Question to reflect on:

How will you set aside a strong perception of your beliefs to get a different perspective?

Connecting through stories and mindful leadership

JOURNAL SPACE

The garden path

Where will this path lead you?

Focused Moments

SECTION FOUR:
SCIENCE IN THE REAL WORLD

In 1999, MIT professor Margaret J. Wheatley, PhD, wrote Leadership and the New Science, introducing how natural sciences explain organizational life. For example, how the aurora borealis mimics organizational communication or how the flowing water in a moving creek or river is akin to achieving the mission. It highlights how we're all connected through a maze of natural phenomena. We've expanded on this work by including over-pressurization, pulleys, and the stress of wind.

Focused Moments

Pascal's Law and Teams
The Theory of Equilibrium

If natural science can explain communication and vision, physics can explain what happens in an over-pressurized environment.

Pascal's law: principles of equilibrium.

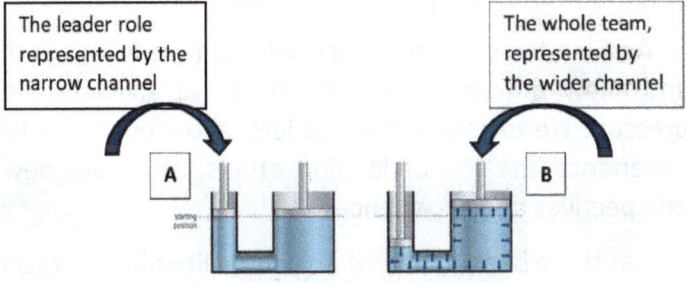

In an optimal environment, healthy pressure is equally applied to everyone on the team, leaving the team to function as expected, as Figure A represents. When an external force -in this instance, the stress or anxiety of the formal leader is unnaturally applied through role compression- the overall balance becomes upset. Figure B represents the manager doing everyone's work but not the work of managing or leading. The force from the smaller area (the leader) is multiplied by the surface area, thereby exerting more significant pressure overall, in this case, the team. The

---

[16] Applying Pascals law to team dynamics. Original image retrieved 3/18/2024 from http://bit.ly/4gcSHzl

increased pressure causes an upset amongst the team, in this case, a pressure cooker in which no one is happy.

When the pressure is in balance, the entire system functions as intended and is in balance. Or, using the adage, many hands make light work. When a leader begins to feel the demands of stress and anxiety, that is precisely when they should allow the team to jump and help, alleviating the pressure overall.

As a leader, we sometimes need to take a step back and allow the team to lead. Thus, we alleviate the pressure we experience as leaders, allow our team to experience the joy of leading others, and gain new perspectives and experiences.

Has there been a time when you realize now that you should have stepped away and allowed someone else to lead on your behalf?

Discussion questions:

1. Sometimes, leaders take on too much work. This creates frustration and stress for everyone. Has there been a time when you have taken on too much work, and what was the result?

2. At what times has your "bucket" been too full? How did you release some of the stress or tension so you could find time to recover?

"Compassion is a verb."

– Thích Nhất Hạnh

By Way of the Water

Goldsboro Creek is in Shelton, WA and runs through a small property handed down from my great-grandmother.

You can see that within the same space, there are places where the water flows very quickly and others where it is very deep and calm; it's quite a paradox. As you think about the white water that occurs as the result of change, consider the spaces with deep pools of calm and stability, and remember that despite what feels like chaos, there is always order. Welcome to science; it is part of our world in many ways.

JOURNAL SPACE

When you think about organizational life, what does the white water and the deep pools of calm represent to you?

_____

_____

_____

_____

_____

Where or how do you find calm as a means for reflecting or finding resilience to step back into the chaos?

_____

_____

Connecting through stories and mindful leadership

How can you use the speed and vigor of the white water as a means to provide you with the energy and stamina to build and/or maintain momentum?

Photo: Goldsboro Creek, Shelton, WA. Photo: Danielle Lord, 2013

Focused Moments

JOURNAL SPACE

The Four Seasons: Spring

What is your favorite part of Spring?

_____
_____
_____
_____
_____
_____
_____
_____
_____
_____
_____
_____

On a mission
An excerpt from Leadership and the New Science

"What is it that streams can teach me about organizations? I am attracted to the diversity that I see, to these swirling combinations of mud, silt, grass, water, and rocks. The stream has an impressive ability to adapt, to change the configurations, to let the power shift, to create new structures. But behind this adaptability, making it all happen I think is the waters need to flow. Water answers to gravity, to downhill, to the call of the ocean. The forms change, but the Mission remains clear. Structures emerge, but only as temporary solutions that facilitate rather than interfere...streams have more than one response to these structures; otherwise, they'd be no Grand Canyon; the Colorado river realized that there were many ways to find the ocean rather staying broad and expansive." (Wheatley, M., 1999, pp. 17-18).

Adapted from Wheatley, M.J. (1999). Leadership and the new science: discovering chaos in a chaotic world. Berrett-Koehler Publishers, San Francisco, CA.

JOURNAL SPACE

A former manager, Susan, claimed she was like a "dog with a bone" regarding specific issues. This is particularly true when something bumps up against our own goals, mission, and values. When were you a "dog with a bone," like the water flowing to find a solution?

_____
_____
_____
_____
_____
_____
_____
_____

Discussion questions:

How do you find the ocean in a sea of stress, frustration, or obstacles?

Do temporary structures interfere with or facilitate your mission?

JOURNAL SPACE

Your summer destination: beach (salt water), lake, or river? What will you do when you get there?

A Little Stress is Vital for Survival

Biosphere 2 is an Earth system science research facility established in 1991 in Arizona. The original was developed in 1987. Both included a variety of botanical species meant to demonstrate the viability of closed ecological systems to support and maintain human life in outer space as a substitute for Earth's biosphere. The biosphere-atmosphere created the perfect environment where the trees were disease-free. Everything, except for one, was accounted for in the biosphere to mimic life in a pristine environment.

Several months into the project, everything was thriving except the trees. Although the trees grew more rapidly than trees outside the biosphere, they fell over before reaching maturation. Numerous botanists and other natural scientists were consulted. After analyzing the root system and bark layers, it was determined that the lack of wind caused a deficiency of stress wood. The lack of stress, through wind, eliminated the trees' ability to develop a natural stress response.

Stress wood forms when "small cracks are formed in the tree's outer layer under stress, which usually occurs from wind." Highly beneficial, the stressed wood helps trees position themselves for optimal sun absorption and grow more solidly. The absence of stress wood allows the tree to grow more quickly, but it cannot fully support itself and will topple and die before it reaches its full growth.

While a life without stress may seem appealing, stress is a life force that develops grit and resilience. A small amount of stress is beneficial to every living being. It helps us develop our human stress wood, ensuring we remain strong during life's storms.

https://en.wikipedia.org/wiki/Biosphere_2

Discussion Questions:

1. How have life stresses given you grit and determination to overcome challenges?

2. In the event of significant challenges, how do you maintain enough of yourself to tackle the tough challenges without becoming jaded or overly negative?

3. Is resilience limited to humans? Why/Why not?

Adapted from The Necessity of Stress.

JOURNAL SPACE

The Four Seasons: Autumn

What is your favorite autumn activity? What emotions does it evoke?

Many Hands Make Light Work:
The history and necessity of the pulley system

A pully is a simple machine consisting of a wheel with a groove in its circumference, a role or cable that runs through the groove, and some type of load (i.e., bricks, buckets) attached to one end of the rope. When one end of the rope is pulled downwards, the load on the other is pulled upwards.

A pully can be limited to one pully or multiple pulleys working as a system,

Multiple pulleys help to distribute the mass and weight of the load,

Functioning together, the system works to multiply the force overall by changing the direction of the applied force.

The more rope wrapped around the pulley wheel, the easier it is to lift the load when working alone.

Working alone, a pulley system is a great asset, providing many hands. Working as part of a team, however, those pulleys are your fellow colleagues' hearts, minds, and hands. Thus, the power of many contributes as a system to move figurative or literal mountains.

Discussion Questions:

1. If we think of pulleys as people, how do you care for or nourish your pulley system?

2. Have you created your own "pulley" system of self-support to minimize human interactions or self-preservation?

3. If there has been a time in which you relied on many hands, what was that experience like? How did you feel about having help, even if it was a simple task?

Focused Moments

JOURNAL SPACE

The Four Seasons: Winter

Snow? Yes, or no? Why?

_____
_____
_____
_____
_____
_____
_____
_____
_____
_____
_____

SECTION FIVE: MINDFUL LEADERSHIP

Much has been written about how mindfulness belongs (or doesn't, some may say) in the workplace. The following pages suggest guidance for facilitating mindful meetings, short meditations for leaders and teams, ten ways to be more mindful at work, compelling questions for team meetings, and journal space to let your ideas flow.

Focused Moments

Definitions

Mindfulness is about paying attention to your present experience with openness and curiosity. It is about being self-aware, more preceptive and curious, responding instead of reacting, staying focused on what's important, and connecting deeply with yourself and others.

Mindfulness is NOT about stopping your thoughts. This will never happen because the brain will do what the brain does: think and process information. It's also not about tuning out but rather tuning in and being more self-aware. Passiveness is also not part of being mindful; it's more about actively engaging in the present moment, tuning into your breath, feeling your feet on the floor, and focusing on various bodily sensations or sounds around you.

Meditation is an exercise that increases your capacity to be mindful throughout the day. It is typically a more formal effort that entails intentional sitting on a cushion (such as a zafu or zabuton) or on a chair, focusing on an anchor like the breath, sounds, or other bodily sensations.

We often hear "soft skills" to describe people with a higher emotional intelligence quotient. (EQ). However, nothing is "soft" about being self-aware, an active listener, and attuned to one's surroundings. These are strengths that leaders should continuously strive to increase, and mindfulness can help enhance emotional intelligence.

Leaders can embody a mindful leadership style by utilizing practices that bring out or enhance self-awareness and situational awareness. Mindful leadership can also help bring a team together toward a common purpose.

For example, when beginning a team meeting, take a few moments to settle into the virtual or in-person space and encourage everyone to take a few deep breaths. Letting go of what has occurred in the past and tuning into the present moment will help everyone, including yourself, focus on the current agenda.

The following pages provide various ways to begin a meeting or a work event with a mindful presence.

Mindful Meetings
Present Moment Awareness

Guided Meditation

"Take a few minutes to arrive and get comfortable. Put your phone down, close your emails, and gently rest your hands on the desk or on your lap. Take a few slow, deep breaths. See if you can feel your feet on the floor. Feel your back resting against the chair.

Now, breathe normally. Let the body do what it does naturally. As you breathe, focus on the in-breath and the out-breath. Maybe you notice sounds in the room. Without identifying what they are, just notice them.

As thoughts arise, as they will do, let them pass by like clouds drifting across the sky. Notice that you are thinking, then let it go and bring your attention back to your breath, or to sounds, or to the feeling of your feet on the floor.

[sit in silence for a minute or two]

Now, bringing your attention back to the space, open your eyes, wiggle your fingers and toes, and let's start the meeting. Thank you for finding your present moment awareness."

Journal Space

"Let go of your mind and then be mindful. Close your ears and listen!" - RUMI

_____
_____
_____
_____
_____
_____
_____
_____
_____
_____

The S.T.O.P. Practice

Haven't there been times when you just needed some "breathing space"? This practice provides a way to step out of automatic pilot mode and into the present moment.

It allows you to create a space to reconnect with your natural resilience and wisdom. You are simply tuning in to what is happening right now without expecting any particular result.

S—Stop what you are doing. Bring yourself into the present moment. Notice your thoughts, feelings, and sensations.

T – Take a breath. Gently direct full attention to breathing, to each in-breath and each out-breath as they follow, one after the other.

O—Open and observe what is happening in your body. Where do you feel tension? Notice what is going on around you. Expand your awareness outward, noticing sights, smells, sounds, posture, and facial expressions…

P – Proceed with new possibilities. This is where you make a choice. How will you move forward from here? There are no expectations.

www.palousemindfulness.com

Journal Space

A resilient flower.

Take a few deep breaths... When you think about an effective leader, what qualities come to mind?

R.A.I.N. for Radical Self-Compassion

Originally created by Michele McDonald and made famous by Tara Brach, RAIN helps direct our attention to find greater clarity. This can help cut through confusion and stress.

R – Recognize what is going on for you in the moment. (Note that the opposite of this is delusion). Make a mental note of what you are most aware of in that moment.

A—Allow the experience to be there, just as it is. (The opposite is resistance.) Let your thoughts, emotions, and feelings be there without trying to fix or change them.

I – Investigate with kindness what it is about. (The opposite is obliviousness). What do you notice in your body? How does this feel in your body? Notice what wants attention and what you believe in that moment.

N – Nurture with self-compassion. You will naturally want to be more compassionate toward yourself when you recognize suffering in whatever form that takes. How can you be intentional in giving yourself comfort? Soften and open your heart.

https://www.tarabrach.com/meditation-the-rain-of-self-compassion/

Focused Moments

"In the end, just three things matter: How well we have lived, how well we have loved, how well we have learned to let go."

– Jack Kornfield

Connecting through stories and mindful leadership

Journal Space

What do you love most about the rain?

"Some moments are like gentle rain, bringing renewal and peace. Others are storms, challenging and intense. Mindfulness invites us to embrace it all, knowing every drop is part of our unfolding."

– Tara Brach

Mindful Walking

Mindful Walking is a powerful and versatile practice that strengthens focus and can be practiced anywhere. It can be the key to moving from the formal practice of meditation to living mindfully every day. There are many ways to practice mindful walking, including as formal practice, informally as you go about your day, or as a longer intentional walking activity. This practice is offered as an informal mindful walking meditation. In addition, doing this regularly will support bringing mindfulness more naturally to our day-to-day lives.

We must take breaks throughout the workday to maintain a healthy work-life balance. Moving mindfully is a beautiful way to do that because it helps you stay more in tune with your body and feelings. Some potential benefits include increasing the ability to focus on tasks and reduce distractibility, increased awareness of internal sensations and external surroundings, regulation of stress, anxiety, and depression, increased capacity to see nuances of the present moment and allowing for better decision-making and self-regulation.

Try this mindful walking activity on your break, whether it's 10 minutes or more. You can do this inside or outside.

To begin, find a walking lane where you have space to take at least 6-10 steps. If you are outside, you will probably be less limited. Your hands can be where they feel most comfortable, at your sides or clasped in front of you. Eyes relaxed and softly looking ahead.

Rest your attention on the breath that is flowing in and out of your body. As you breathe, be aware that you are breathing. Pay attention to each in-breath and each out-breath.

Be curious about the sensations you feel while standing. Notice the pressure of your feet on the floor or the earth, the alignment of the bones, and the position of the hips. Just be aware of standing.

As you become ready to move, notice the weight shifting from standing on both feet to adjusting your body to one leg as you lift the other to take a step. Note any sensations of lightness or heaviness. Begin slowly walking forward. You might time your steps with your breath. Take one step forward on the in-breath and another step forward with the other foot on the out-breath or whatever rhythm feels most comfortable.

Move at a pace that is comfortable and accessible while maintaining the ability to stay present. When you notice your mind has wandered, gently and kindly bring your attention back to the soles of your feet and the sensations of walking.

As you do this activity, remember that you are not trying to get anywhere. Not even to the next step. You are just arriving in the present moment, step by step.

When you are ready to proceed with your day, take a few deep breaths and thank yourself for taking the time for a mindful walk.

"Do not underestimate the power that comes to you from feeling the simple movements of your body throughout the day.

~ Joseph Goldstein

Cultivating Compassion

This practice is designed to cultivate compassion and kindness for oneself and others. However, it's different from other practices in that participants are invited to engage with the mind to help generate feelings of compassion and kindness. You may have seen this called the loving-kindness practice, or Meta (Pali word), and this version has the most appropriate language for a workplace setting.

I invite you all to let go of whatever you were doing or thinking about before now and drop into the present moment by taking a deep, full breath in through the nose, holding onto that breath for a few seconds, and then slowly exhaling until your lungs are completely empty.

You can do this one or two more times at your own pace, closing your eyes if comfortable or lowering your eyes with a soft downward gaze.

Returning to normal breathing, the invitation now is to bring to mind someone for whom you have feelings of warmth, kindness, love, or gratitude and repeat these phrases to yourself:

May you be happy
May you be healthy
May you be at peace

May you be safe

If your mind wanders off into other thoughts, kindly and gently, without judgement, come back to the present moment and repeat the phrases again.

May you be happy
May you be healthy
May you be at peace
May you be safe

Now, letting that focus go and re-directing those same sentiments to yourself and repeat these phrases silently to yourself:

May I be happy
May I be healthy
May I be at peace
May I be safe

Bring kindness to whatever you notice. And giving these sentiments to yourself one more time.

May I be happy
May I be healthy
May I be at peace
May I be safe

Now, I invite you to bring to mind your community. Widen the circle as much as you can. And repeat these phrases silently to yourself.

May you all be happy
May you all be healthy
May you all be at peace
May you all be safe

Now opening your eyes, coming back to the room, taking a nice big stretch if that feels good.

Thank yourself for your practice.

Focused Moments

"As soon as you honor the present moment, all unhappiness and struggle dissolve, and life begins to flow with joy and ease."

— Eckhart Tolle

10 Ways to be More Mindful at Work

1. When walking around the office, deliberately notice the sensations of your body moving, your feet touching and leaving the floor with each step, and the little things around you that you didn't notice before.

2. Don't criticize yourself for having irrational emotions. Give yourself grace, notice the emotion, and let it go.

3. Notice when your mind wanders, and gently bring it back to the present moment. Notice your breath or a touchpoint on the body, maybe where your back touches the chair.

4. During lunch, eat mindfully. Intentionally notice the food's texture, smell, and sound. Savor every bite, chew your food thoroughly and notice how you feel.

5. Notice how your foods and drinks affect your thoughts, bodily sensations, and moods.

6. Every hour, stand up, stretch, change your gaze. Mindful movement during your workday will help you focus and relieve stress.

7. If distressing situations or thoughts arise, practice S.T.O.P. When you take a moment to pause, breathe, and observe, you can proceed with new possibilities.

8. Schedule time to slow down if you feel rushed throughout the day. Sometimes, self-care needs to be on the calendar.

9. Know your limits. Taking on too much and always saying yes can harm your health. It's okay to say, "I'd love to take that on, but I'm maxed out right now."

10. Look outside, or better yet, take a stroll outside if that's accessible, and notice visual elements in art or nature, such as colors, shapes, textures, or patterns of light and shadow.

Mindful Questions for Team Meetings

Sometimes called "ice breakers," asking a mindful question encourages more profound thought for a more robust conversation. Often, we begin meetings by asking how everyone's weekend was or if they have anything fun planned for the next one. While these are great conversation starters, they only touch the surface of what could be an opportunity for a deeper conversation. Depending on the purpose of the meeting, asking mindful questions can help the group transition from where they were before the meeting started to the present moment. That is the crux of experiencing a focused moment.

10 Mindful Questions

Here are some questions to encourage thoughtful introspection and offer opportunities for meaningful dialogue, helping team members connect through shared vulnerability and authenticity.

1. What's one small thing you've done recently that brought you joy or made you feel accomplished?
2. What is one piece of advice you would give yourself at the start of your career?
3. Describe a simple habit or ritual that helps you stay grounded during busy days or stressful times?
4. What's a recent act of kindness—big or small—that you experienced or witnessed?
5. If you could describe your current mindset or energy as a weather pattern, what would it be and why?
6. What's one challenge you've faced that helped you grow in ways you didn't expect?
7. Can you share a moment when you felt truly aligned with your purpose?
8. If you could share a piece of wisdom from a book, podcast, or someone you respect, what would it be?
9. What's something you've learned about yourself through working with others?
10. What's a question you've been pondering lately, and how has it shaped your perspective?

Make your own list of mindful questions to use as a resource for your team meetings.

Focused Moments

ABOUT THE AUTHORS

Focused Moments

DANIELLE

Author and Pacific NW native Danielle Lord loves Washington State for its misty winter mornings, the beaches of Puget Sound, and the colorful native rhododendrons that dot the spring landscape.

Danielle is passionate about leadership and bringing compassion through leadership to organizations of all sizes. Organizations have existed in an outdated managerial paradigm for too long, and with it comes limiting beliefs and mindsets that stifle creativity and kindness. We can do better for our team members.

With 30 years of experience in organizational development, Danielle has seen remarkable transformation through leadership development. Having earned her Ph.D. in Leadership Theory in 2007, she has designed, developed, implemented, and managed Leadership Development at the enterprise level for Providence Health and Services, the State of Washington, and the Port of Seattle. She has a passion for innovation and continues to look for unique ways for employees to excel in organizations.

Governor Gary Locke (2003) and Senator Maria Cantwell (2004) recognized Danielle for her contributions to innovative work in healthcare development. She has also received the Outstanding Faculty Award from Brandman University (2014), the Governor's Innovation Award for Leadership Development (2017), and the Woman's Outstanding Achievement Award for Leadership Development (2020).

A self-described *"China-phile"* and Jasperware junkie, Danielle is a partner in a Vintage Rental company and a lifestyle blogger featuring beautiful tables. She lives in the Puget Sound area with her husband, Stephen, where they enjoy gardening, antiquing, and wine.

Danielle is also the author of Engaging Your Employees: 12 Heart-Centered Strategies to Drive Your Organization's Culture & Commitment (2024).

ANIKA

Anika is a seasoned HR professional with a passion for fostering leadership development and promoting mindfulness in the workplace. She holds advanced degrees in Organizational Leadership (ORGL) and Human Resources Management (HRM), alongside an undergraduate degree in sociology.

Through Joy House Publishing, LLC, Anika supports first-time authors and co-authors' stories that teach children about mindfulness. She is also a Mindful Change Coach with Hälsa Coaching for Mindful Living, a Certified Workplace Mindfulness Facilitator, and is on a personal journey to becoming a Certified Meditation Teacher.

Throughout her career, Anika has led initiatives prioritizing employee well-being and professional growth. These include designing a comprehensive mindfulness program, establishing a mentorship platform for government employees, and managing wellness and recognition programs that foster team engagement and emotional intelligence. Her dedication to the transformative power of mindfulness is evident in the workplace programs she has developed, integrating meditation and mindful movement to create a kinder, more connected organizational culture.

Connecting through stories and mindful leadership

HOW TO CONTACT US

Danielle Lord
Archetype Learning Solutions
www.archetypelearningsolutions.com
Email: danielle@archetypelearningsolutions.com

Anika Klix
Hälsa Coaching for Mindful Living
www.halsacoaching.com
Email: anika@halsacoaching.com

Billie Frances
Guiding Mindful Change
www.guidingmindfulchange.com
Email: billie@guidingmindfulchange.com

TESTIMONIALS

"I like how you can open up the book on any page and find a story, image, or question that provokes thought or dialogue. This book is part journal and part treasure trove of short vignettes to unite people in shared experiences and focused moments. Love it! I will use it as a resource at my staff meetings!"

- Amazon Review, A Seattle-lite

"A great, inspirational read."

-Robert Ingram, author: The Genius Who Saved Baseball

"People are desperate for connections. Focused Moments provides the opportunity to connect with others in new ways. I've used this book with my dementia clients to engage them meaningfully."

-Lucy Rau, Dementia Caregiver

"One of my favorites. I highly recommend it."

-Mary West, Founder of the Mary West Network

www.ingramcontent.com/pod-product-compliance
Lightning Source LLC
Chambersburg PA
CBHW070539170426
43200CB00011B/2470